D0060221

Printed Under License ©2017 Emotional Rescue
www.emotional-rescue.com

Published by Studio Press
An imprint of Kings Road Publishing. Part of Bonnier Publishing
The Plaza, 535 King's Road, London, SW10 0SZ

www.bonnierpublishing.co.uk

Printed in Italy   10 9 8 7 6 5 4 3 2 1

The Wit & Wisdom of
THE WIFE

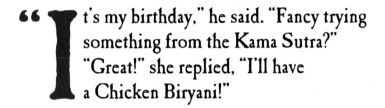

"It's my birthday," he said. "Fancy trying something from the Kama Sutra?" "Great!" she replied, "I'll have a Chicken Biryani!"

She didn't care if her outfit was uncomfortable and rather odd looking — it was an expensive designer label, and that was all that mattered.

nstinctively, she understood that if God hadn't wanted women to have lots of shoes and handbags, why would he have given them arms and legs?

She was suffering from the old 'Woman's Problems'...
Not enough wine and chocolate!

Her shopping trolley was a lot like her husband. Difficult to control and mostly full of booze and fatty foods.

he knew exactly what turned
her husband on,
which was why she'd
filled the bath with lager.

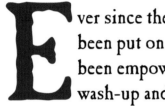ver since the strange metal band had been put on her finger, she had been empowered to continually wash-up and cook meals.

Her husband said he'd got her a present that would make her knickers wet.

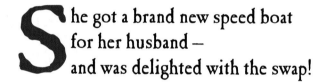

She got a brand new speed boat
for her husband —
and was delighted with the swap!

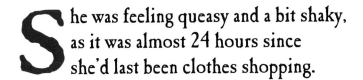

She was feeling queasy and a bit shaky, as it was almost 24 hours since she'd last been clothes shopping.

er hubby's promise to give her multiple earth-shattering orgasms had really moved her... She hadn't laughed that much in ages!

He could tell she had dialled the wrong number, she'd stopped chatting after only 25 minutes.

Naturally, she made sure she was fully-prepared for her birthday night in!

He wondered if his wife had packed enough clothes for their weekend break.

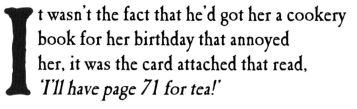

It wasn't the fact that he'd got her a cookery book for her birthday that annoyed her, it was the card attached that read, *'I'll have page 71 for tea!'*

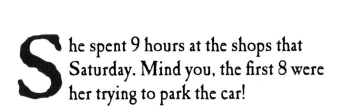

She spent 9 hours at the shops that Saturday. Mind you, the first 8 were her trying to park the car!

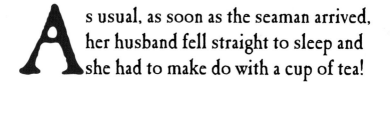

As usual, as soon as the seaman arrived, her husband fell straight to sleep and she had to make do with a cup of tea!

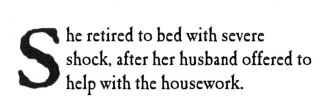

She retired to bed with severe shock, after her husband offered to help with the housework.

ust hearing the words 'chocolate' or 'shopping' would send her into immediate orgasm.

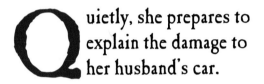

Quietly, she prepares to explain the damage to her husband's car.

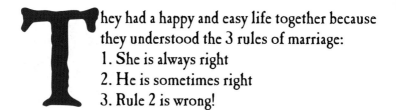

They had a happy and easy life together because they understood the 3 rules of marriage:
1. She is always right
2. He is sometimes right
3. Rule 2 is wrong!

The slightly parted lips, the longing in the eyes; yep, it was their anniversary and she wanted it real bad... but enough about chocolate!